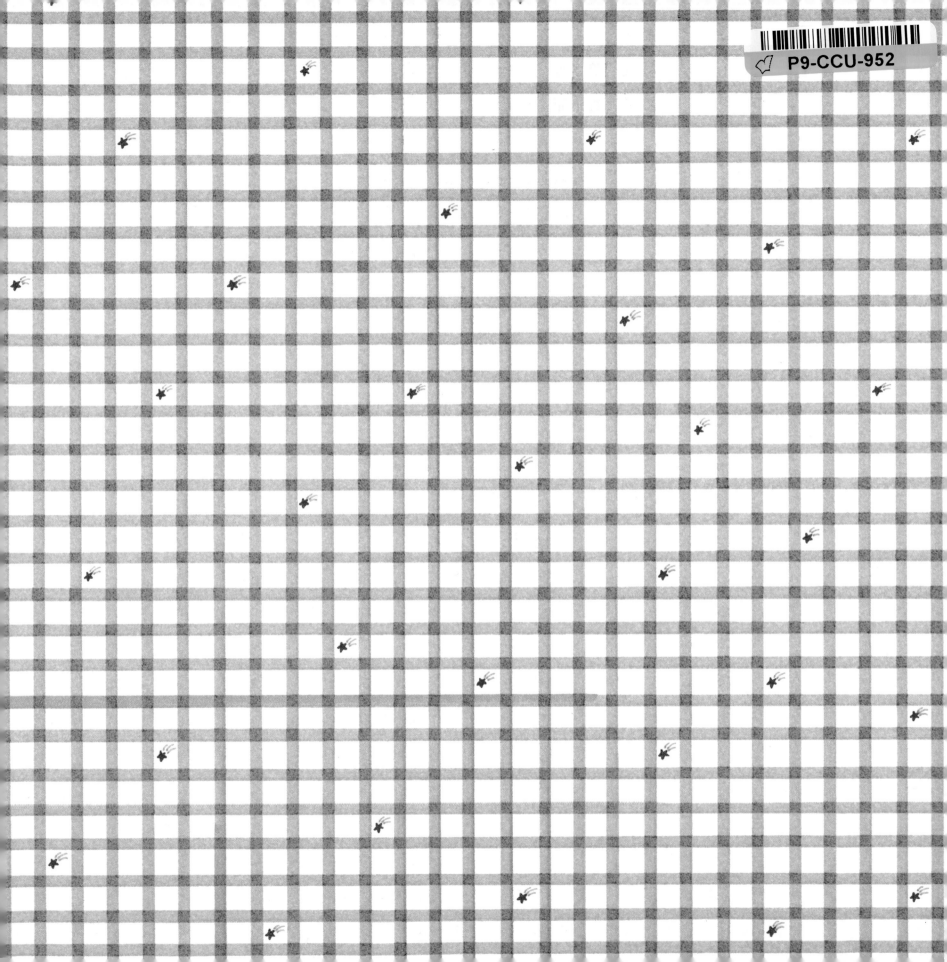

Mary Engelbreit's
Christmas Companion

Mary Engelbreit's
Christmas Companion

The Mary Engelbreit Look and How to Get It

Illustrations by Mary Engelbreit

Written by Charlotte Lyons

Photographs by Barbara Elliott Martin

Andrews and McMeel

A Universal Press Syndicate Company

Kansas City

10 9 8 7 6 5 4

Library of Congress Cataloging-in-Publication Data

Engelbreit, Mary.
    Mary Engelbreit's Christmas companion : the Mary Engelbreit look
and how to get it / illustrations by Mary Engelbreit ; written by
Charlotte Lyons ; photographs by Barbara Elliott Martin.
       p.   cm.
    ISBN 0-8362-4627-6 (hc)
    1. Christmas decorations. 2. Handicraft. I. Lyons, Charlotte.
II. Title.
TT900.C4E53   1995
745.594'12--dc20   95-19426
                                          CIP

Design by Stephanie Raaf

Contents

Introduction...7

1 Bringing in the Season...9
Project: Kitchen Wreath...17

2 Down the Chimney...19
Project: Felt Stocking...33

3 O Christmas Tree...35
Project: Felt Tree Skirt...47

4 Merriment...49
Project: Decoupaged Plate & Painted Glass...59

5 Tabletop Trees...61
Project: Forest Angels...71

6 All Through the House...73
Project: Papier-mâché Santa...93

7 Traditions...95
Project: Christmas at Our House Album...109

8 In the Wink of an Eye...111
Project: Appliquéd Sweater...121

Project Patterns...123

Credits...134

Introduction

Mary and Santa, 1954.

I think about Christmas all year long! I have to think about it in order to create new designs for my greeting cards. Of course, I'm always hoping to come up with a new best-selling design to out-do last year's. This can be a real challenge in the middle of July, but whenever I get stuck, I know where I can turn for help. I get out all of the wonderful Christmas decorations that I collect year-round—and believe me, there are plenty of them!

I can always find a spark of inspiration in my Christmas collections—a favorite ornament, a snapshot of the boys on Santa's lap, or a cherished memory from my own childhood. Christmas is an extraordinary time when the meaning of even the simplest experience becomes magnified and enchanted. By recalling Christmases past, I keep in touch with that holiday spirit.

And what better way to provide warm memories for your family than by turning a corner or nook of your home—or an entry or tabletop—into a Christmas wonderland. The magic of the season will sparkle in your home and in the eyes of all who share your holiday with you. Decorating the home for the holidays is one of my favorite pursuits. The children love to help—especially when it comes to the tree. They have their favorite ornaments to display front and center—and each ornament has a past and story that goes along with it.

I love collections and it's easy to work them into my holiday decorating. My Santas, snowmen, reindeer, and miniature evergreen trees are easy to find spots for, but it's also fun to find new ways to use other things I love—like teapots full of holly, old toys brought down from the attic to sit and visit around the tree, and old quilts as colorful tree skirts. Thinking of ways to use everyday objects to celebrate the joy of the Christmas season is a great part of the fun.

In this book, Charlotte, Barbara, and I have tried to capture for you the spirit of the Christmas holiday as we see it. When you look through these pages, imagine the crunching snow, the breeze of angel's wings, the laughter of Santa as he sails above the rooftops. We hope that our work, and the work of like-minded folks whose wonderful houses are also pictured here, will motivate you to create your own magic at home—put your elves to work! But most of all, we want you to remember to have fun—don't let Christmas become a chore—and best wishes from all of us!

Mary Engelbreit

For our children—
Will, Maggie, Libby, Zooey, Maury, Evan and Erin

chapter one

Bringing in the Season

**"Glad tidings of great joy I bring
To you and all mankind."**

—Nahum Tate

The thrill of Christmas is one of those secret pleasures that lingers in our hearts throughout the year. Each fall when the air first chills, we cannot wait to jump in and get busy. Treasured decorations, held in storage, come tumbling out in profusion and glorious array. Opening the boxes is like Christmas morning itself. Old favorites, wrapped in sentimental memories, spark stories of holidays past and inspiration for yet another Christmas beginning. This is the season that renews our family ties, our winter spirits, and our affection for our homes.

Decorating the house is a joyous effort that brings together all ages, from the toddler who rearranges the tree's lowest branches to Grandmother needlepointing the newest stocking. What better place to begin decorating than the front door? Whatever you hang—a wreath or a child's artwork—your front door is a signal to the world that the celebration of Christmas is at work inside. Certainly there is nothing like the pungent fragrance of fresh evergreens to stir the holiday senses, but outdoor decorations made from unconventional materials are charming, too. Look around you with a creative eye. Whatever strikes a festive note will work as long as it suits the surroundings and the season.

Mary's front door
enthusiastically announces
that this home loves Christmas
and all its playfulness (opposite).
Small toys and ornaments
are wired into a wreath
that encircles a nutcracker with a crisp,
checkered bow.

11

Charlotte's house is dressed
in arbor vitae cuttings
from a neighbor's fall pruning (left).
Paper houses
nestle in the boughs (below).
The small crabapple heart,
hanging to the left of the wreath,
was simple to make
by stringing fall apples
on floral wire,
bending to shape,
and air-drying.

Fresh fruits are simple adornments
used over the traditional door
of this handsome beach house (opposite).
Decorating for the holidays in warmer climates
is a challenge that sparks inventive ideas.

Woodland garlands drape the door of this old farmhouse in the country.
Threaded gold ribbon crowns a decoration
easily made with a few basic materials.
Beginning with a star fashioned from styrofoam,
the center is padded with a thin layer of moss to build it up.
Another layer is added using floral pins.
Wrap the finished piece in gold braid and hang.
Simply splendid!

Sentimental mittens are a sweet addition
to this door decoration (below).
The house dedication etched in stone above the door
closes its message with a carefully chiseled heart.

A checkered front door
gleefully beckons Santa's reindeer
with an enticing bunch of carrots (above).
When there isn't a chimney,
Santa has to know which door
to come in.

Giant nutcrackers made in art class
at school usher in the season.
Indeed, as you walk through this neighborhood,
you'll spot where all the kindergarten artists live
when you see variations of the nutcracker
hanging on their doors.

Handmade Christmas

Kitchen Wreath

Dress up your kitchen door or window with this colorful and inventive decoration. An Italian specialty food shop offers the best selection of interesting cans, jars, and pastas.

Materials:

- One fresh evergreen wreath
- One dish towel
- 3 wooden spoons
- Miscellaneous products and produce from the kitchen
- Fresh parsley
- Floral wire
- Wire cutters
- Acrylic paints and brushes

How To:

Determine where the wreath will hang from the back and solidly wire a hanger at that point. Tie the dish towel in a loose knot so that it resembles a big bow. Cut a length of wire to feed through the back of the knot. Wire it to the wreath at the top. Paint the handles of the wooden spoons in a variety of patterns and colors such as dots and stripes. When dry, wire these into the bottom of the wreath. The products chosen for the wreath pictured here are 4 cans of tomato paste, 2 heads of garlic, 3 nests of angel hair pasta, 3 sweet red peppers, 1 jar pesto sauce, and a jar of artichoke hearts. Make and twist wire loops around the tops of the cans and jars. These must be very secure because they are so heavy. Run lengths of wire through the garlic heads, pasta nests, and peppers. Arrange the ornaments around the wreath and wire securely into place. Garnish with sprigs of fresh parsley and basil wherever desired.

**"The ornament of a house
is the friends who frequent it."**

—Ralph Waldo Emerson

chapter two

Down the Chimney

"Oh! holly branch and mistletoe,
And Christmas chimes where'er we go,
And stockings pinned up in a row!
These are thy gifts, December!"

—Harriet F. Blodgett

The magical wonder of a Christmas stocking hung by the fire touches each of us, no matter what age. Made just for that special someone—from lace, yarn, quilts, or felt—stockings are unfailing reminders that we are uniquely remembered by another. Once hung, the stocking seems to burst with the anticipation of all the celebration to come. And, at last, who can forget the feel of tiny gifts bulging through the seams as it is lifted down into anxious hands?

At the mantel—Santa's doorway—decorations add to the focus and expectations of Christmas. It is the perfect place for collectibles that tell a family tale—toys from childhood, silly Santas gathered through the years, heirloom glass ornaments too precious to float in the tree. Nestled among greens and candles, the glass glimmers with the nostalgia of Christmases past. In the same way, arrangements of fresh flowers, fruit, and garlands of ribbon combine with the firelight to nourish the senses and inspire the season. This is where the children will line up for photographs, where Grampa may read a yuletide classic, and where your friends will warm their hands before the party begins.

A turn-of-the-century fireplace is dripping
with family stockings both old and new (opposite).
Guarding each is a skinny Santa.
Dolls and bears from every child's room
get together for Christmas tea.
Funny how the cookies are actually eaten up!

21

The shallow dining room mantel
is cleverly built out with an extra board (below).
Disguised with layers of folded paper doilies,
it is now deep enough to display greens
and "new-like-old" collectible ornaments.

A tray of light awaits guests
in this supremely Victorian entry (above).
Richly appointed with antiques such as the Austrian candelabra,
English needlepoint panel, and store-bought ancestors,
the room is lavishly embellished with
gold-leafed magnolia leaves and fresh gardenias.
The domes shield works of waxed fruit and flowers
made by Victorian girls at finishing school.

Mary's living room mantel becomes a brilliant showcase for a collection of tree toppers.
At eye level they can be admired in full splendor, alone or together.

Nutcrackers and Santas
line the shelves of a parlor fireplace (below).
Crocheted pillow trim and folded linen napkins
bring with them a bright, snowy look.
A retired gentleman spent an entire year
carving the Santa center-front.
Indeed, the carver entered a craft fair
with only one finished piece
and this collector was lucky enough to find it first.

In a woodland cabin, a natural stone fireplace provides a cozy place
to array greens, candles, and dried flowers (below).
A snowstorm is welcome here,
if it means staying at home before the fire.

Cinnamon-colored walls banish the wintry chill
where comfortable hours are spent before the fire with Lily,
a Cavalier King Charles Spaniel (opposite).
Berried eucalyptus, heather, and lilies bank the marble mantel
while freshly cut sprays of evergreen
crown the Hungarian painting above.

Trimmed simply with a forest of small trees,
the diminutive Navajo nativity is a favorite decoration,
alongside the banded totem sticks made by children
using markers and string (left).
Beaded Native American boots in the colors of Christmas
take the place of traditional stockings.

An unassuming mantel
simply leans against a wall here,
but still offers a place to hang stockings
fancied up with buttons and bows (right).
The dollhouse rooms are packed
with Christmas characters this season.
Such an eclectic mix of furnishings and decorations
provides a fun-loving comfort,
especially at Christmas.

Cockscomb, heather, statice, and cedar weave a woodsy garland
across the mantel of a great room addition.
The arrangement begins with two large baskets
to anchor the display.

Handstamped with black and gold linoleum cuts, the deeply hued wall
highlights the abundance of color in the floral decorations.
The antique mantelpiece is ablaze with fresh oranges, pyracantha, and winter berries.

A stone cottage mantel is brimming with spruce and pine
in this spacious living room where china and sterling
gleam among lovely antiques.
Even the bookshelves are dappled with snippets
of cedar and holly.
Baskets of greens are nearby
for fragrance and last-minute additions.

Handmade stars
are stuffed with good wishes
and wrapped with vintage trims (below).

These stockings, made from damaged crazy quilts,
bring a timeless appeal to the mantel draped in greens cut from the backyard (below).
Mixed in here and there are old green pottery pieces,
collected from garage sales over the years.
Their muted shades of green echo the faded fabrics.

A collection of roosters
lend their cheer
to a sitting room mantel (opposite).
Colorful and funky,
the addition of evergreens and
wrapping paper is enough
to launch anyone's holiday spirit.

All the toys saved from Mary's sons' younger years
revel in the seasonal spirit when they greet each other again
on the mantel and below.
Father Christmas has the attention of children Evan and Will,
in these companion portraits.
An antique ferris wheel, perhaps an old store display fixture,
holds small gifts in each seat and becomes an irresistible gathering place
for any visitor—especially younger ones.

Handmade Christmas

Felt Stocking

Materials:

- 2 pieces black felt, 18" x 12"
- Colored scraps of felt in red, green, yellow, brown, lavender, dark green, and white
- Gold sequins
- 1 foot of 1" black and white gingham ribbon
- 12" jumbo red rickrack
- 12" green ball fringe
- Red pearl cotton thread and embroidery needle
- Glue or HeatnBond

How To:

Enlarge pattern, shown on page 123. Cut two stocking pieces according to the pattern, one for the front and one for the back. Cut out felt shapes according to the pattern and apply to one of the black felt pieces for the front. Use glue or HeatnBond to apply. Add trims across the top of the stocking as shown in the photograph. Wrap raw edges of trim to the inside of the front stocking. Add sequins. With the top facing you, place the back of the stocking underneath the front, careful to line up the edges. Pin and machine top-stitch together, leaving an open top. Blanket stitch with pearl cotton all around the sewn edges of the stocking. Finish with a loop at the top for hanging.

"Heap on more wood! The wind is chill;
But let it whistle as it will,
We'll keep our Christmas merry still."

—Sir Walter Scott

chapter three

O Christmas Trees

"There's a dear old tree, an evergreen tree,
And it blossoms once a year.
'Tis loaded with fruit from top to root,
And it brings to all good cheer."

—Luella Wilson Smith

Every year we head for the tree lots or the country in search of the perfect tree. Sometimes we find it right away— sometimes there doesn't seem to be one. But most trees just need to be fussed over enough and they'll be radiant, even though imperfect. Any tree is transformed by the flicker of light, the shimmer of glass, and the power of sentiment.

The ornaments that work the greatest magic are the ones that have a story to draw us near. Paper dolls from childhood, seashells from a honeymoon, baby spoons— anything from the past, really. The things that make a family special animate a Christmas tree as well. Making your own ornaments year after year adds to the scrapbook feeling that connects one Christmas to another—the glimpse of your teenager studying a clay ornament made in preschool brings forth the seasonal nostalgia we long for. Some part of the tree ceremony should involve tradition. It could be a family trip to the tree lot, a brunch for the trimming, or a late-night gathering of friends for ornament crafting. When Christmas is over, and the tree absolutely must come down, invite everyone back to help with the task and then stay for a cozy winter supper.

A child's (or collector's) dream-come-true tree is festooned with Steiff stuffed animals (opposite). For thirty-five years this tree has delighted children and grandchildren with the ever-growing menagerie.

37

Strong branches hold animals
that have been secured
with green floral wire (left).

In a home where no detail is overlooked, Christmas offers the chance to enhance every corner once more.
Fringes, majolica, and chintz unite with garland, crystal, and lace for an intricate loveliness.
Among traditional furnishings, the old-fashioned tree with its colorful decorations
combines with buttery walls and paperwhite porcelain to give the feeling of an English country house.

Mary's hall table becomes a central pedestal for her Christmas tree wrapped in a storybook felt skirt.
Children's ornaments and family favorites are carefully chosen for their whimsical appeal.
Simple swags of greenery with huge crimson bows entwine the stairs.

Handmade ornaments include
a celestial tree topper carved from styrofoam,
dipped in plaster, and finished
with gold spray paint (below).
The crown is cut from a cardboard tube,
painted with acrylics,
then sparked with sprays of wire and stars.

At the windows, generous swags of silk
hang from forest branches
holding fallen nests
and other natural accents (above).
Best-loved ornaments are those made
with friends over the years.

Antique toys fill the space
beneath this glorious tree (opposite).
The stone farmhouse is radiant at Christmas
when timeworn heirlooms gleam in the spirit
of the season.

Outfitted with old souvenir dolls from garage sales
and ornaments made by her children,
Charlotte's tree is topped by her handmade doll—turned angel—
with quick wings fashioned from a folded doily (above).
A piece of bent wire supports the fold.
Daughter, Erin, painted the snowflake plaid carton,
then lined it with batting for an ornament keepsake box.
Each year she makes a new one as a gift for her mother.

The glass ornaments
and the ribboned plastic fruits
adorn a live tree
nestled in a weighted clay pot (left).
Traditional and yet contemporary,
it is displayed in the entry
leaving more room in the living room
for entertaining.

The garlanding on a stairway
is lavished with seeded eucalyptus
and winter berries (above).
Cascading fruit echoes the ornaments
on the potted tree.

This hall tree is brimming
with vintage hats, bags, and gloves (below).
Victorian calling cards draw us closer
into the enchantment.

Strings of flags and other Scandinavian crafts crisscross this tree
whose sparse branches beautifully display larger ornaments (above).
This year's tree didn't meet with everyone's approval,
but it literally followed them home on the arms of children
who pleaded its virtues all the way to the car.
What could they do but go back and pay for it?

When two sisters
broke up their doll clothes collection,
they couldn't remember which mitten pair
belonged to which sister (right).
So, as a compromise,
they made two mixed pairs
and a promise to keep them together always.

Sentimental pieces from childhood,
such as a church offering envelope,
are some of the surprising
ornaments on this tree,
but it tells a family story to children
when they decorate each year (above).
The hang tag from the Cabbage Patch doll
is there, too, as a remembrance
of the long wait in line
that mother endured
for that essential gift.

A vintage Barbie sweater
hangs from a miniature hanger (left).
Doll clothespins make perfect hangers
for small ornaments.

Handmade Christmas

Felt Tree Skirt

Materials:

- 2 yards of 60" black craft felt
- 1 yard of 60" green craft felt
- Squares or small yardages of felt in red, brown, white, yellow, gold, turquoise, tan, gray, magenta, lavender, blue, dark green
- 7 yards of red ball fringe
- 2 yards of HeatnBond fusible fabric glue sheet or white glue
- Scissors, iron, safety pin, string 36" long, and chalk

How To:

Lay out black felt, folded, on a table or floor. At the center of the fold, pin a length of string with the chalk tied to one end. The tip of the chalk to the pinned end should measure 30 inches. Draw a halfcircle, using the string as a guide. Shorten the string to 3 inches and draw an inside halfcircle to cut away for the trunk. Cut through both thicknesses to make a round circle that is 60 inches across. Cut the inside circle away, leaving a 6-inch opening. Before opening the fold, mark off 6 equal panels (3 on each side) for 5 storybook designs and one plain hilltop.

With the green felt, cut 6 green hills according to the pattern found on page 124. Using HeatnBond or white glue, bond hills (leave 1/2 inch of the top edge unglued) to the bottom edge of the black skirt so that they create an overlapping hill and valley landscape all across the skirt. The sixth hill is split in half through the center when you make a straight cut from the bottom edge to the trunk opening. This will be the back.

Transfer the house patterns to felt and cut exactly to size. If using HeatnBond, apply it to the whole square of felt first, and then cut shapes from pretreated felt. Following the manufacturer's instructions or using glue, bond houses and other designs to black felt. Whenever possible, slip lower edge of house, tree, or evergreen under the edge of the hilltop. On the sixth panel, add trees and shrubs. Go back and glue down the open edges on the hilltops. Glue small yellow stars to the sky and a red pointed collar to the trunk opening. Trim the bottom edges of green and black felt to get a clean edge and handstitch red ball fringe all around.

"There is no instinct like that of the heart."

—Lord Byron

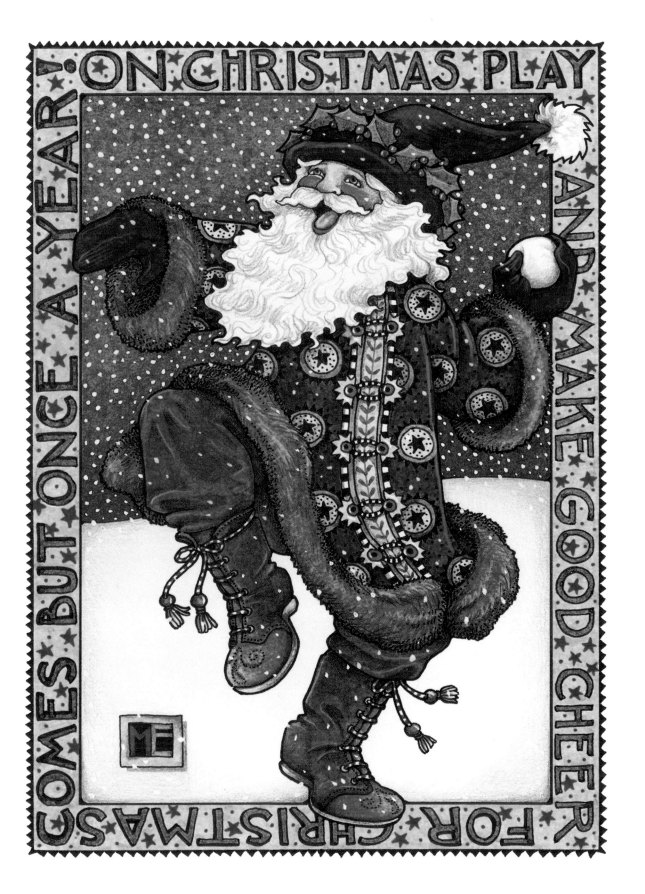

chapter four

Merriment

"Small cheer and great welcome makes a merry feast."
—William Shakespeare

The holiday season is as much about food as it is about decorations and gifts. What would a celebration be without the welcoming table prepared for a holiday feast? We love to be fed and feted—and this is the time when friends drop by casually, children linger at home, and everywhere we look the spirit calls us to merriment.

Simple tea and cakes take on a new sweetness atop a kitchen table cheerfully sprigged with greens and ornaments. Candles glowing amid colorful linens or vintage fabrics give excitement to everyday dishes. A few pieces of just-polished silver mix in perfectly with fresh fruit and flowers, giving timeless romance to any setting. Perhaps a tiny gift or a clue to a secret Santa treasure hunt beckons each guest to her place. Even a well-used worktable can host chairs decorated with stockings, cards, or drapes of greenery. If you can imagine it, chances are it's worth a try, so open the cupboards and set the table!

■ ■ ■ ■ ■ ■

Lovely throughout the year, the breakfast room already has many ingredients for holiday dress (opposite). A few extras such as stockings at the window and paper houses on the sideboard combine with the tabletop tree to carry the season.

A sunny dining room keeps its warmth for the holidays with the appearance of a wooden evergreen centerpiece,
classic Christmas dishes, and inviting stockings on the chairs.
Towers of narcissus blend with houseplants and make everything seem more Christmas-like.

Everyday dishes
mix easily
with holiday theme cups
and glasses.
Year-round decorative pieces
and Mary's cherished collectibles
welcome the emphasis
on Christmas red and green.
Enjoying this light-hearted setting,
friends can casually gather
for a gift-exchange
over coffee and cookies.

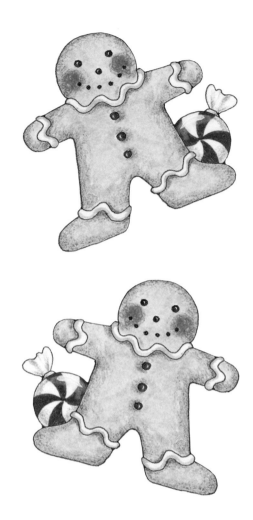

Wildly eclectic and fanciful,
this dining room goes crazy with Christmas.
The table mixes rustic Adirondack-style chairs with crystal,
tinsel, and heirloom Belleek china.
Grapevines and a tree of forest-found antlers give
the feeling of a wonderland celebration.

Minton plates stand out vividly beside pyracantha,
winter berries, and ranunculus (left).
A chandelier is cleverly fashioned
from clothesline, candles, berries, and prisms.

Boxwood, holly, roses, and gardenias
come together to form an opulent table decoration (right).
Silver and Staffordshire fill the huntboard
with elegant formality
while cranberry glass casts a rosy glow
throughout the afternoon.

Christmas curios watch over a table
set with black pottery dishes and an angel
whose face is a delicately painted acorn (below).

Illuminated by an old chandelier turned upside down for a different look,
golden stars and plaid ribbons cascade toward the table
set with party crackers and crystal (above).
The blue and white export china punctuates the panelled walls.

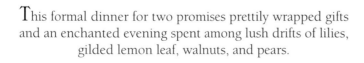

This formal dinner for two promises prettily wrapped gifts and an enchanted evening spent among lush drifts of lilies, gilded lemon leaf, walnuts, and pears.

Inviting the charm and color of Christmas trimmings,
the dining room table is set for Christmas Eve
when stockings full of goodies adorn each chair (below).
Individual snowmen await each guest
and the crystal bowl gleams
with the simplicity of glass ornaments.
There can never be too many decorations—
this is a good way to use the surplus.

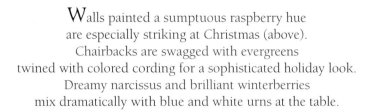

Walls painted a sumptuous raspberry hue
are especially striking at Christmas (above).
Chairbacks are swagged with evergreens
twined with colored cording for a sophisticated holiday look.
Dreamy narcissus and brilliant winterberries
mix dramatically with blue and white urns at the table.

Handmade Christmas

Decoupaged Plate & Painted Glass

Materials:

- Clear glass plate
- Drinking glass
- Liquitex® Glossies paints
- Brushes
- Assorted Christmas cut-outs and stickers
- White paint
- Mod Podge® or vinyl wallpaper paste

How To:

For the plate, arrange the cut-outs and stickers on the back, facing up through the glass for a pleasing look. As much as possible, cover the entire plate wth images. All the work is done on the underneath side of the plate. Paint the face of each cut out with Mod Podge® and apply to the plate back. Cover the entire surface in this manner. When dry, paint the back of the plate and cut-outs with white paint to fill any gaps in the decoupage. Apply at least two layers of Mod Podge® over this.

For the glass, use the glossies to paint the outside with dots, bows, and other Christmas designs. Bake in the oven according to the directions on the paint product. Take care when washing these. They are mostly for decorative use and will not stand up to constant use.

"A rule for happiness—
Something to do,
Someone to love,
Something to hope for."

—Kant

·THE CHRISTMAS GARDEN·

61

chapter five

Tabletop Trees

**"The whole world is a Christmas tree,
And stars its many candles be."**

—Harriet Blodgett

Not every room can accommodate a glorious seven-foot evergreen, but a smaller tabletop tree stands in as a joyful alternative. Made from silk, grapevine, or the real thing, a little tree dresses up so easily with a handful of tiny decorating scraps. Choose a theme that's right for a room or begin with a collection of small things already there. What's in your gardening shed or your child's toy box?

Consider a friend's hobby and scoop up trinkets to fit a tree that's designed just for him. Dollhouse miniatures offer lots of possibilities for decorating a wee tree. Try making your own trimmings from bakeable clay or from odds and ends found at home. Hot glue and wire are handy tools for the assembly, since you'll need to tuck little things into the branches. Unusual crocks and containers work well as bases to hold the tree in place and give it visual strength. As a table centerpiece, or even in a quiet corner, a little tree holds its own very nicely, attracting a fair share of admiration just because it is small.

A dining room corner is devoted to this little tree
and the charming arrangement it inspired (opposite).
The stack of ribbon spools takes away
that "don't touch" feeling
and encourages anyone to take a closer look.

Mary's tabletop tree is absolutely out of this world.
Space ships and robots clutch every branch and a rocket blasts off the top.
Set into a tin bucket filled with nuts and bolts from the hardware store, it was as much fun to make as it is to admire.

Amusing wooden cut-outs, wrapped empty boxes,
and sections cut from plastic garland beads,
dangle from branches
on this cleverly animated tabletop tree (below).

A feather tree makes the most of collectible ornaments,
showing each to its best advantage (above).

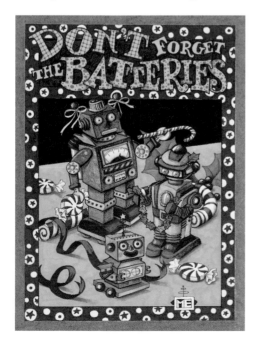

In the kitchen,
a playful little tree
is flanked by topiaries
and delicious
culinary efforts.
At Christmas,
everyone works together
in the kitchen,
side-by-side,
on whatever the
occasion calls for—
whether it's cookies
or canapes.

Charlotte's hand-painted clay pot holds a craft tree ornamented with small birds, twig-framed sketches, and gardener's tools.
The sketches are penciled onto heavy paper then colored and framed with hot glue and twigs.
Easy-to-use acrylic paints band the pot.

As if each of these Santa's packs were emptied out for this tree,
countless toys and trinkets are hotglued onto a mesh cone.
The entire concoction was spray-painted gold
for an unusual collage tree.

Charlotte's thirteen-year-old friend Anna
provided the fascinating toothpick people for this little tree (below).
She makes them out of notebook paper, sequins, beads, and toothpicks.
There's a toothpick artist holding a palette of sequins
and a skater has little skates made from bent staples!

A garage apartment has all the charm of a garret
with its dormered rooms and gothic windows (above).
One niche is the perfect backdrop for this little tree.
A galaxy of heavenly collectibles does the trick.

This miniature tree is trimmed with dollhouse chairs,
spray-painted gold and upholstered with fabric scraps (below).
Beaded garlands are wrapped around rosettes
made from ribbons, and a broken charm bracelet
provided small ornaments that are used as glittering faux-jewels.
Again, a few simple materials used imaginatively
dazzle the eye.

A woodland fantasy tree
brings the forest inside with painted mushrooms
and natural accents (above).
The birchbark box is a perfect choice for a rustic base.

Handmade Christmas

Forest Angels

Materials:

To make one angel:

- 2 pieces of 18" craft wire
- 1/4 yard muslin
- 6" x 10" print fabric for dress
- Tulle netting scrap for petticoat
- 1 skein (8 yards) Persian yarn needlepoint wool for hair (or other soft yarn)
- Polyester stuffing
- 8" white paper doily for wing
- Sewing threads in red, blue, and white
- Red colored pencil

How To:

To make the wire form for the angel's body, see the complete instructions and diagram on page 131. When the form is completed, mummy-wrap the legs and arms with muslin strips that have been torn into 1"-wide lengths. Fold these in half lengthwise, so that the folded edges show on the wrap and the torn edges are concealed by the wrap. Wrap toward the tip of the hand or foot, and then go back over the first wrap. When the wrap reaches the neck, tie a knot. Twist wire to tighten wraps.

Stuff the stuffing into and over the wire loop on the head. Cover with a 5" square of muslin. Adjust gathers toward the back of the neck, so that the face is as smooth as possible. Wrap the gathered muslin several times at the neck with a length of white thread. Sew the faces, shown using colored threads, according to the face pattern on page 131. Use a red colored pencil to make nostrils and blushed cheeks.

Place the center of the wrapped arm wire at the neck back. Wrap each arm around the neck one full time as you would a neck scarf. Arms should come from the back when complete. Cut a small neck hole and make a slit in the center of the dress rectangle to fit over the doll's head. Put the dress on the doll as you would a poncho, keeping the slit in the back where the doll's hair will cover it. Stitch the neckline of the dress to the doll, so that the fabric fits close to the chin. Gather the material at the waist, tucking it under the arms, and secure with thread. Fold over the raw edge of the sleeve cuff and hem. Add a gathered petticoat of tulle over the skirt.

For the hair, use a piece of cardboard cut to 4-1/2", wrapping the yarn around it four times. Cut the loops at one end of the yarn

and lay it across the doll's head. Stitch each piece of hair in place down the center of the head using thread that matches the hair. Continue with 4 or 5 more shanks to back of neck. Cut four, 1" pieces of yarn for bangs and stitch each in place. Tack the hair down around the face and at neck. Cut remaining yarn in uneven lengths to layer over the first layer of hair. This creates fullness and a natural look.

For the wings, pinch the doily fully across the center to form a bow-tie shape. Sew the pinched center to the top of the doll's back. Let the hair fall over the wings at the back. Bend legs and arms to flying pose. Use thread to make a loop for hanging at the back of the neck.

"Novelty is the great parent of pleasure."

—Robert South

chapter six

All Through the House

**"We are the music-makers
And we are the dreamers of dreams."**
—Arthur William Edgar O'Shaughnessy

Decorating for Christmas is such fun that it spills over into every room of the house. In the kitchen, where much of the celebration starts and finishes, casual decorations find their way to sills and shelves, wreaths dangle from windows or odd spots—a small tree sports the year's favorite cut-out cookies. Other rooms show signs of the season with overflowing ornaments or fresh flowers and greens lending fragrance to the air. A tray of candlelight or a border of votives always contribute magic and tiny vignettes of collectibles invite thoughtful attention.

Favorite greeting cards, saved from the year before and inexpensively framed, can transform a hallway into a gallery. Consider devoting a whole room to the display of Christmas elves or mix decorations among year-round furnishings that you already have and cherish. Let the holiday infuse your home with the unusual spell it creates. Though it's only here for a short while, it gives us a winter full of warmth.

■ ■ ■ ■ ■ ■

In Mary's sunroom,
a luscious wreath fills the winter view (opposite).
Reindeer of all kinds collect on the sill
behind the welcoming window seat.
A fitting portrait creates a backdrop for the vignette.

This kitchen wreath
is made from deciduous huckleberry
and lightweight plastic fruit
(opposite).

The colors of the season are freshly chosen in a kitchen
where the exuberance of ranunculus, yellow roses, and cymbidium orchids
merges with pomolos and other fruits to create a feast for the senses (above).

Mary's vast collection of Santas
greets carollers from the top of the piano in her library (above).
An antique, tree-shaped postcard holder brings a variety of greetings
to the scene while vintage children's books are easily retrieved
from the plate rail above.
Mary often looks to the covers for inspiration in her own work.

A nativity fills this piano corner with a seasonal grace.

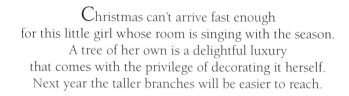

Christmas can't arrive fast enough
for this little girl whose room is singing with the season.
A tree of her own is a delightful luxury
that comes with the privilege of decorating it herself.
Next year the taller branches will be easier to reach.

Redecorate a wall with seasonal artwork
such as framed greeting cards
or a shadow box full of tiny holiday ornaments (below).

Mary vibrantly repainted this old reindeer shelf
and, after wondering what it was once used for,
found that it nicely holds votives at the window (above).

A Christmas sticker turns into a tie pin
when combined with matboard and trim (right).
In between wearings, the tie and pin decorate a dresser mirror
with a holiday note.

This tranquil sitting room
is devoted to the elves and their feather tree (below).
Even the window molding bears a trim or two.

Another spot for Christmas stockings
is right on the bedroom door (above).
This also serves as a great distraction on Christmas morning
when earlybirds find it hard to wait for the sleepy grown-ups.

A natural wreath
of dried flowers
and nuts
hangs over open shelves
of the secretary.
The English chairback
worked in beads
and needlepoint
contributes to
the holiday elegance.

A collection
of glass character ornaments
has grown to a grand number
during this collector's lifetime.
Although he doesn't always
put up a tree,
he can't resist bringing them out
each year.
The French daybed
covered in silk damask
barely holds the lot.

85

A house built of floral mosses and trims
seems the perfect home
for the Christmas elves (below).

*S*antas slip into any available slot on this library bookshelf (above).
Clearing the way meant putting away other treasures,
but the holiday display succeeds with the help of small houses and reindeer.

Charlotte's entry table showcases a collection of Santas gathered through the years.
Mary's gift of an M.E.- style Father Christmas is the extraordinary focal point.
Tins and a little tree create varying stages for small arrangements within the larger one.

Gift tags saved from long ago childhood gifts
mix with current ones to sprinkle the staircase garland
with a profusion of special memories (opposite).
A handpainted Christmas handkerchief fills the easel
and Santas of every age greet visitors.

Baskets full of twigs and thistles tower above a table gathering of Santas (above).
Made from papier-mâché pulp, each wears a tuft of cotton bearding
and a spray of berry or evergreen (right).
Their little faces twinkle with all the merriment of Christmas.

LOOK TO THE BEAUTY OF THIS DAY
MIRACLES ARE ALL AROUND YOU

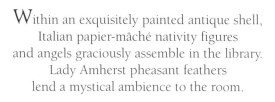

Within an exquisitely painted antique shell,
Italian papier-mâché nativity figures
and angels graciously assemble in the library.
Lady Amherst pheasant feathers
lend a mystical ambience to the room.

Thrift-store stepstools stack up to display
exotic second-hand finds and a créche (below).

English Staffordshire figurines
seem to have stepped right out of the landscape
painted on the nineteenth century screen (above).
Flowering plants and greenery
combine with luxuriant bows for a romantic beauty.

If you don't have a fireplace mantel,
decorate a radiator cover as though it were one (below).
Pedestals hold topiary globes and
ornaments catch the light in a shallow bowl.

Knicknamed "the wealthy aunt,"
this store-bought portrait inspired the wall color
and sideboard still-life (above).
Winterberries, paper whites, and seventeenth century
bronze candlesticks frame the English sterling punch bowl.
Gold-leafed apples and pears mingle with dried orange slices
to complete an exceptional scene.

Handmade Christmas

Papier-mâché Santa

Materials:

- Cardboard (cereal box or poster weight)
- Newspaper
- Masking tape
- Papier-mâché paste (l cup water, 1/2 cup flour, and 1 tablespoon white glue)
- Acrylic paints and sealer
- Brushes
- 4 cotter pins for joints
- Sandpaper
- Drill or awl

How To:

Cut out cardboard according to the pattern on page 132. Build up the body with crumpled newspaper. Leave tips of arms and legs flat when building it up, so that the joints will be flat. Tape paper into place. Begin to layer papier-mâché strips of torn newspapers. Remember to wrap across the back, too. Allow to dry between layers. Make at least three layers of papier mâché. When thoroughly dry, sand rough edges lightly and base-paint white.

Then paint according to the colors in the photo and on the pattern. Seal with acrylic sealer. Don't forget to decorate the back. Drill holes to attach the limbs to the back of the body. Insert cotter pins and bend back to hold. Drill a hole through the hat and thread with string to hang.

**"Home, the spot of earth supremely blest
A dearer, sweeter spot than all the rest."**

—Robert Montgomery

REMEMBRANCE, LIKE A CANDLE·····BURNS BRIGHTEST AT CHRISTMAS TIME

C. DICKENS

chapter seven

"Custom, then, is the great guide of human life."
—David Hume

At Christmas, traditions are the colorful ribbons that tie us all together. Perhaps passed along by another generation or invented just last year, repeating cherished customs or stories in a special way makes every family unique. This is a good time to research your heritage and adopt some of the discovered celebrations or foods. Simply adding to a collection of select holiday ornaments becomes a favorite tradition for collectors. Activities such as seasonal crafting, cooking, and entertaining are customs well-loved by everyone.

Giving gifts of talent, like poems, readings, songs, or a parent's handmade treasure for each child, creates extraordinary memories that reappear fondly in a family's folklore. Children are remarkable family historians— remembering all of the details grown-ups sometimes forget. Each year, let them remind you of the way the holiday is supposed to unfold. We are surprised to see what is considered a tradition in their eyes. Hopefully, it's something more enchanting than Aunt Martha's lumpy gravy at Christmas Eve dinner.

■ ■ ■ ■ ■ ■

A restful way to ease the holiday bustle
is to read Christmas books before the fire as a family (opposite).
After dinner, cookie-making, or shopping,
sharing stories of the season reminds us of the reasons we celebrate.
Before you know it, it is time for *'Twas the Night Before Christmas*!

A summer guest cabin is reserved for teddy bears at Christmas.
Although all the details of their comfort are considered
by the collector who puts the scene together,
it is the hugs from visiting children that give the greatest pleasure.

A Christmas gift that contributes to a collection creates a unique history—especially for a young child.
Snowglobes line up merrily with other best-loved childhood toys.
Those things we hold dear seem to shine especially bright at Christmas.

Handmade gifts for friends
are lined up at the door as party favors
following the annual cookie exchange (below).

If you sew, begin a tradition by making a new outfit
for a child's doll (below).
Imagine the thrill of finding an old friend
magically dressed for the holiday!

During the Depression, a father presented a coconut
as a Christmas gift to each of his children (opposite).
It was enough to bring laughter and
joking to a skimpy celebration.
Every year thereafter, the table centerpiece
is a traditional reminder of that simple gift
remembered most of all as the loving legacy of Christmas.

A fast frame gallery of Santa photographs
provides a little history of Christmas through the years (below).

Making cookies with children
gets right to the real meaning of Christmas—
sweet smiles (left).

Mary and her son, Will, made this nativity set by repainting the old wooden créche and then using bakeable clay to make the figures. Small trees and animals around the house fit in perfectly. Instant heirloom!

103

An old box, painted by a child to represent the holiday, promises a renewed gift of sentiment year after year.

Charlotte and her husband, Andy,
made this theater one Christmas
and it has become a traditional part
of the family's celebration since (below).
Their puppet show makes an exciting finale
to the long wait for Santa.
Off to bed with dreams of the day to come!

Perhaps Santa would like to rest those old bones by the fire
before he goes on his way (left).
A merry table set by the children each year
invites him, at least, to read the note and have a cookie.

Little gingerbread house cookies are glued
to votive candle boxes with royal icing (below).
For a simple house decoration they are festive and fun to make
with friends or children.
They would make sweet party favors, too.

Start a Christmas tradition that's a treat for everyone (right).
How many pieces are in each jar?
Children record their estimates and hope they get it right
because the best guess wins the contents.
Be sure to watch the sticky fingers.

Twelve-year-old Maggie built this village for Charlotte.
Its irresistible charm comes from the mix of twigs, colorful paints, and bottle-brush trees.
After painting the craft store houses, she decorated a scrap-board base and glued it all together.
The fence was certainly the trickiest part, but the glue gun even handled that.
Children love to make their own gifts—sensing, perhaps, how dearly they are cherished.

Little shoes,
handpainted for little feet,
add special excitement
to holiday dress (left).
In the following years,
you may want to add them
to your keepsake decorations.

At a family dinner, each place setting
offers a piece of jewelry
fashioned from grandmother's
cherished button box (right).
A gift, a memory, a treasure!

Handmade Christmas

Christmas at Our House Album

Use a scrapbook to keep track of your special holiday traditions. Decorate the cover with decoupage and fill the pages with notes, recipes, and snapshots of your holiday.

Materials:

- Department store photo album
- Assorted stickers, holiday postcards, old greeting cards
- One file label with red border
- Permanent black marker
- Gold stars
- Spray adhesive, paper glue, or Mod Podge®
- Acrylic sealer and brush

How To:

Arrange cut-outs and stickers on album cover. Glue into place, leaving room for file label in the center of the top. Write "Christmas at Our House" on label with a permanent marker. Apply to front over the design. Glue gold stars into place wherever needed. Apply acrylic sealer or Mod Podge® over the entire surface.

"What an enormous magnifier is tradition!
How a thing grows in the human memory
and in the human imagination,
when love, worship, and all that lies in the human heart,
is there to encourage it."

—Thomas Carlyle

chapter eight

In the Wink of an Eye

"The manner of giving is worth more than the gift."
—Pierre Corneille

As you're moving along your way, remember that quick Christmas tricks can be the most fun. Letting our imaginations run wild leads us to discover whimsical gifts and decorating approaches. Again, we love the unexpected ease that comes with using simple techniques and materials. Christmas doesn't last very long so we have greater freedom to show off our efforts.

Collections, paint, cookie dough, whatever strikes our fancy—tinkering around with these elements kindles great brainstorms. More than anything, make Christmas your own—in the way that you celebrate with those you love and in the delight of sharing the season. We wish you an exceptional Christmas full of euphoric laughter and sweet pleasures to bring you happiness through the year. Be sure to make it merry and bright!

■ ■ ■ ■ ■ ■

Scatter stickers and cut-outs onto a purchased frame
for a special holiday look (opposite).
Add painted polka dots and it's complete.
These would be especially appealing
with old snapshots of Christmas inside.

Thrift shop novels or holiday books
fill out a basket of kindling
for a simple gift (left).
For a family of many ages,
choose classic tales
that can be read aloud together.

An antique copper mold
is paired with a delicate gold-rimmed plate (right).
Embellished with seasonal greens and a recipe tucked inside.
This is an imaginative gift for a cook.

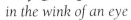

Make these tree ornaments
from chandelier crystals, tulle,
and bent wire.
Using pliers, twist them together
and, suddenly,
their sprightly shapes twinkle merrily.

Kits from the crafts store just await your special touch (below).
Paint a clock with a simple winter scene
and assemble the rest in minutes.
Be sure to sign the back with a gift message.

Although girls of long ago cross-stitched samplers
in their spare time, girls today are busy
with soccer practice and other active pursuits (above).
This project appeals to kids on the go
who have the same sentimental thoughts
and wish to create a gift worth framing.
Colorful markers and pencils replicate embroidery.

Holiday stickers applied to matboard shapes
make clever button covers (below).
The edges are dressed up with gold braid trim
and look right at home on a gift blouse.

"All I want for Christmas is my two front teeth!"
A quick and easy hat is made from polar fleece
and a store-bought pattern (above).
A folksy pin jazzes it up and comes off for style changes.
Polar fleece is soft on both sides
and makes a very wearable hat that doesn't tickle or chafe.

A lovely old bowl brimming with mixed nuts
and a nutcracker makes a charming gift (below).
A fuzzy squirrel and an evergreen sprig
combine with a vintage card
to save the need for giftwrapping.

An old-fashioned tin basket
chock-full of home-baked goodies or tea supplies
carries a gift book of friendship (above).
Inscribed with a personal dedication,
the book is tied onto the handle with a bit of green.

Gingerbread cookies decorated
to resemble family members are too adorable to eat (left).
Use them to animate a family diorama at the table.

A jacket made from an old quilt
takes on extra character with buttons and pins (right).
Sew the buttons on securely
because little hands can't resist their color and clatter.

119

A footstool picks up a Christmas theme with acrylic paints and sealer.
Another instant heirloom to keep near the tree year after year.

Handmade Christmas

Appliquéd Sweater

Materials:

- Navy acrylic sweater
- Red replacement buttons
- 6-inch pieces of polar fleece or washable fabric in red and yellow
- 1/4-yard blue-green polar fleece
- Red acrylic yarn
- Gold pearl cotton thread
- Embroidery needle, pins, and scissors

How **T**o:

Cut out shapes from fleece according to the pattern you have created or copy the pattern pictured here. Polar fleece is like felt and does not need the edges folded under which is necessary with other woven fabrics. (Felt should not be used because it is not washable.) Pin and appliqué your designs to the front using pearl cotton thread and a blanket stitch. Use red yarn to embroider the vines with a feather stitch. Loosely blanket stitch the neckline with yarn, being careful to make an allowance for stretching later. Replace the buttons with new red ones. Decorations can be continued onto the back, if desired, using a garland pattern and making adjustments for fit.

"Blessed are the happiness makers."

—Henry Ward Beecher

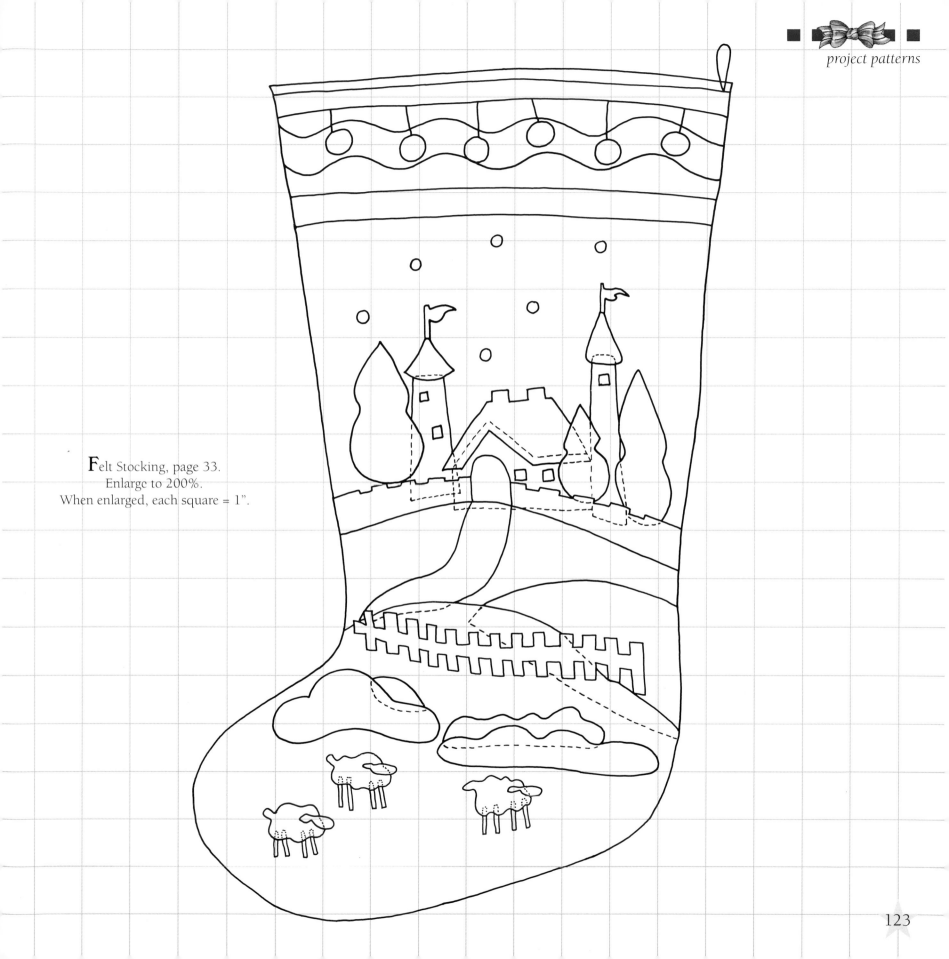

Felt Stocking, page 33.
Enlarge to 200%.
When enlarged, each square = 1".

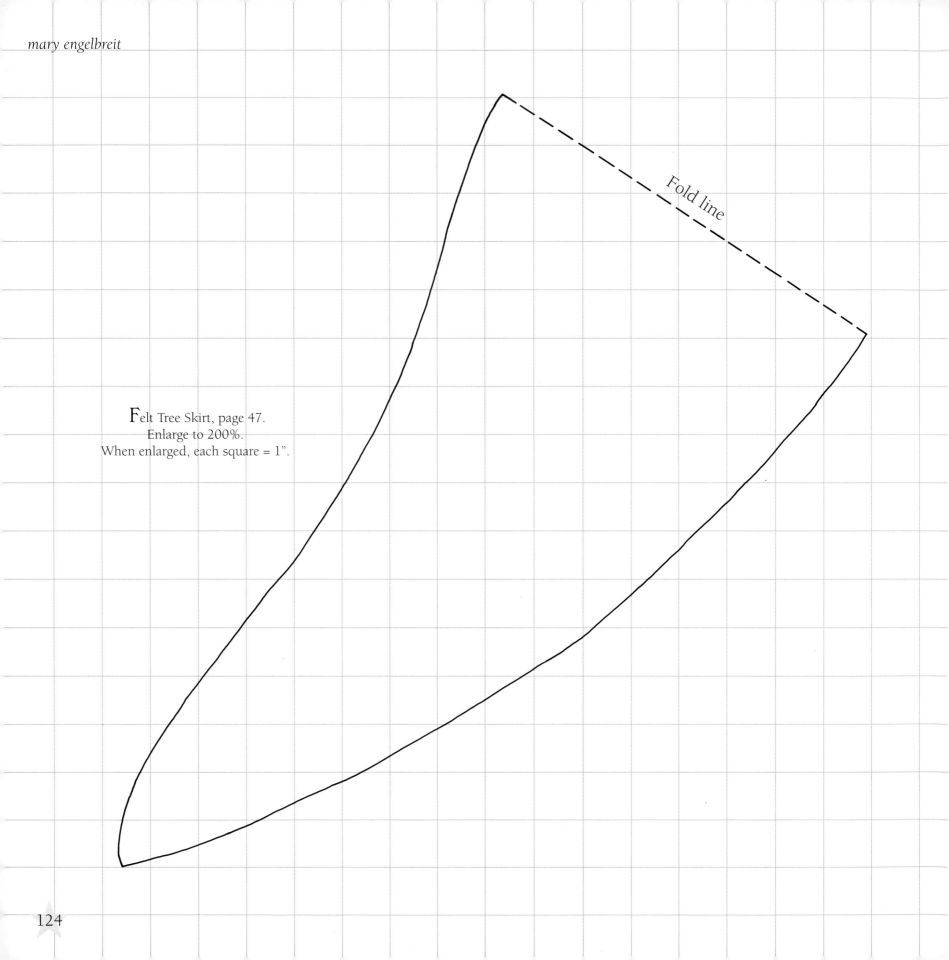

mary engelbreit

Fold line

Felt Tree Skirt, page 47.
Enlarge to 200%.
When enlarged, each square = 1".

124

Felt Tree Skirt, page 47.
Enlarge to 125%.
When enlarged, each square = 1".

Felt Tree Skirt, page 47.
Enlarge to 125%.
When enlarged, each square = 1".

Felt Tree Skirt, page 47.
Enlarge to 125%.
When enlarged, each square = 1".

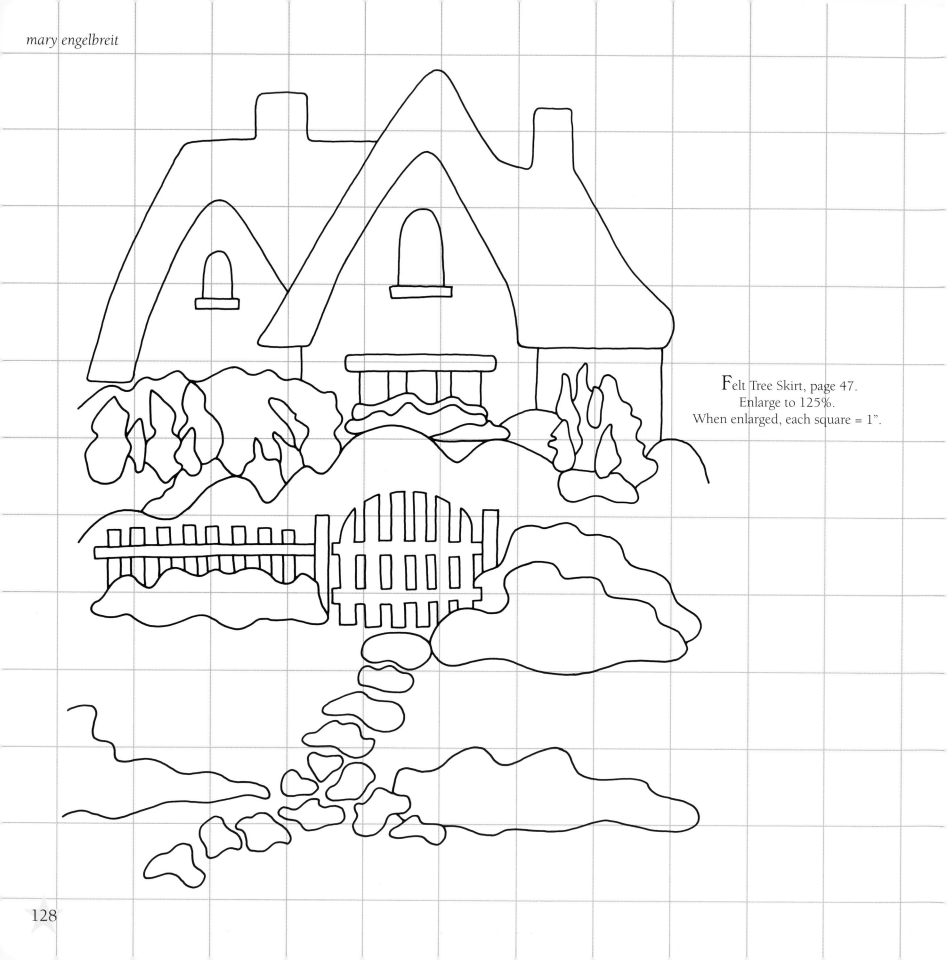

Felt Tree Skirt, page 47.
Enlarge to 125%.
When enlarged, each square = 1".

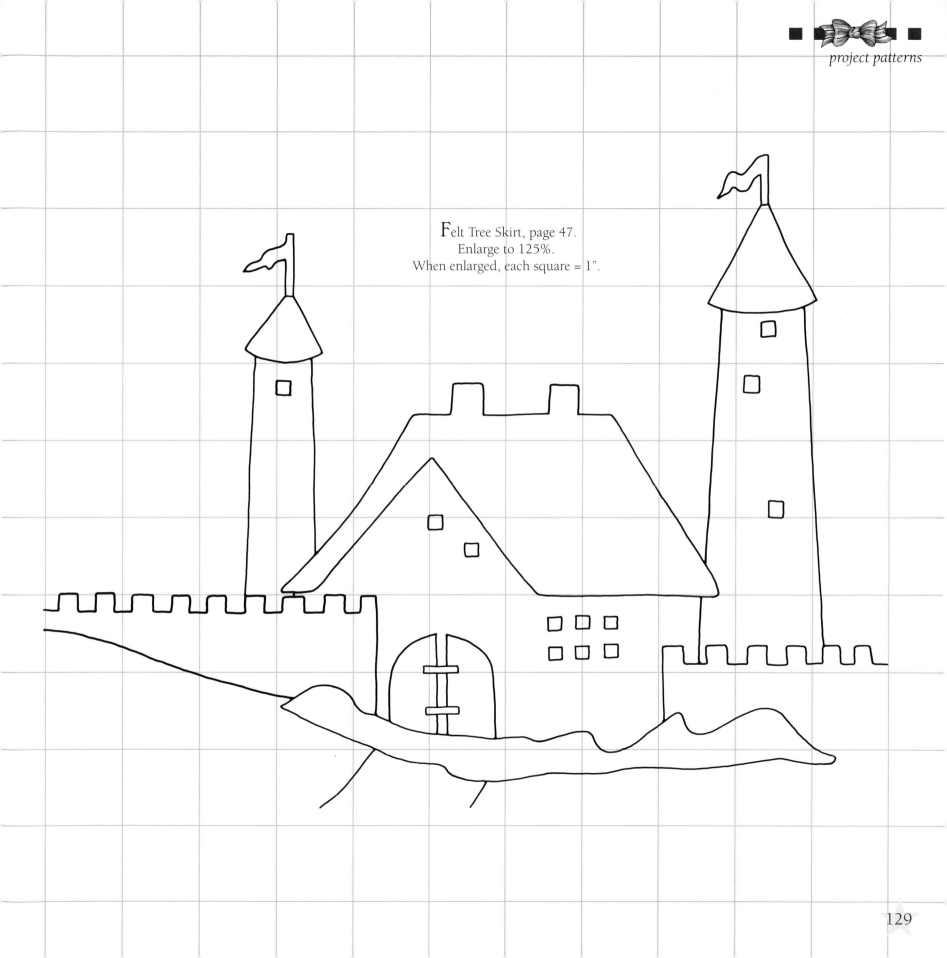

Felt Tree Skirt, page 47.
Enlarge to 125%.
When enlarged, each square = 1".

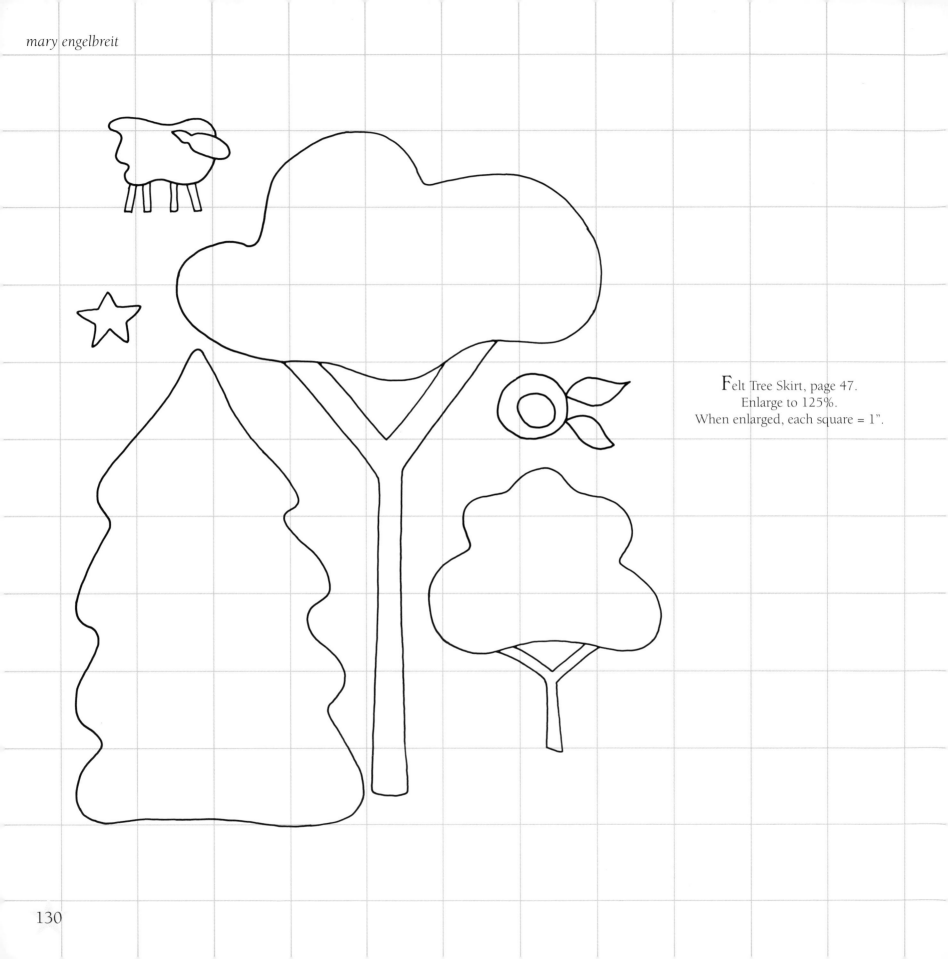

Felt Tree Skirt, page 47.
Enlarge to 125%.
When enlarged, each square = 1".

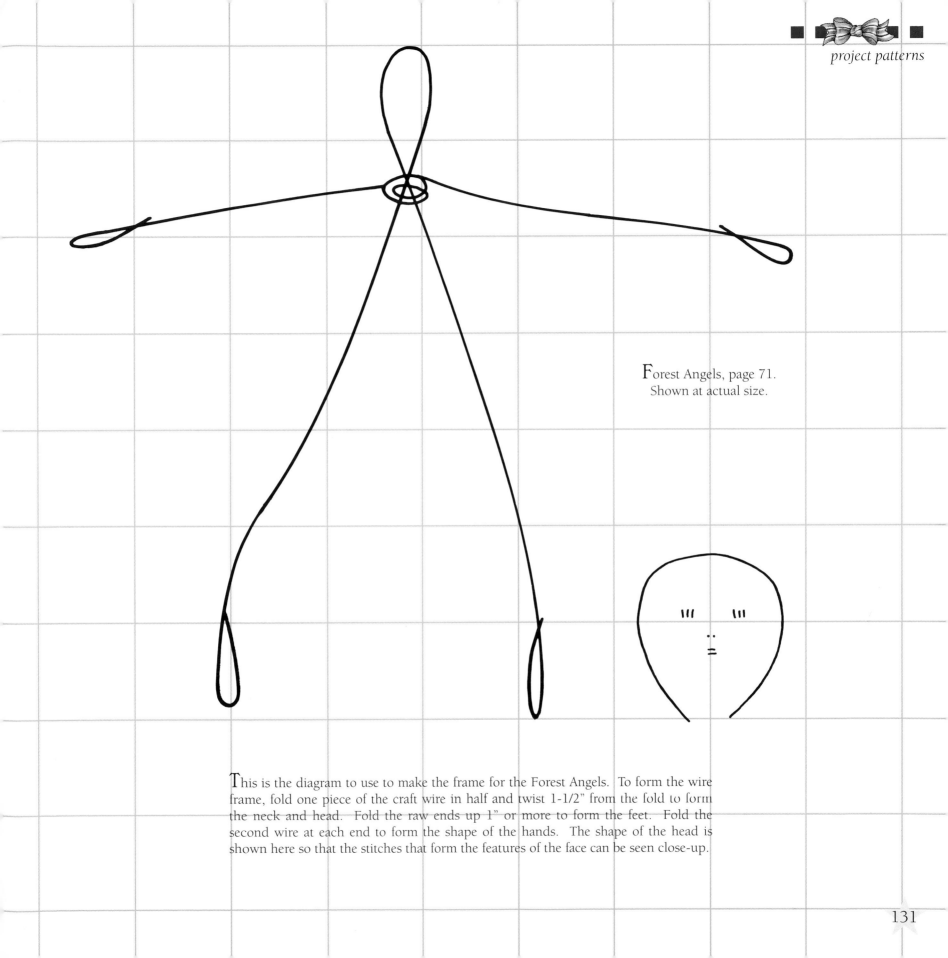

Forest Angels, page 71.
Shown at actual size.

This is the diagram to use to make the frame for the Forest Angels. To form the wire frame, fold one piece of the craft wire in half and twist 1-1/2" from the fold to form the neck and head. Fold the raw ends up 1" or more to form the feet. Fold the second wire at each end to form the shape of the hands. The shape of the head is shown here so that the stitches that form the features of the face can be seen close-up.

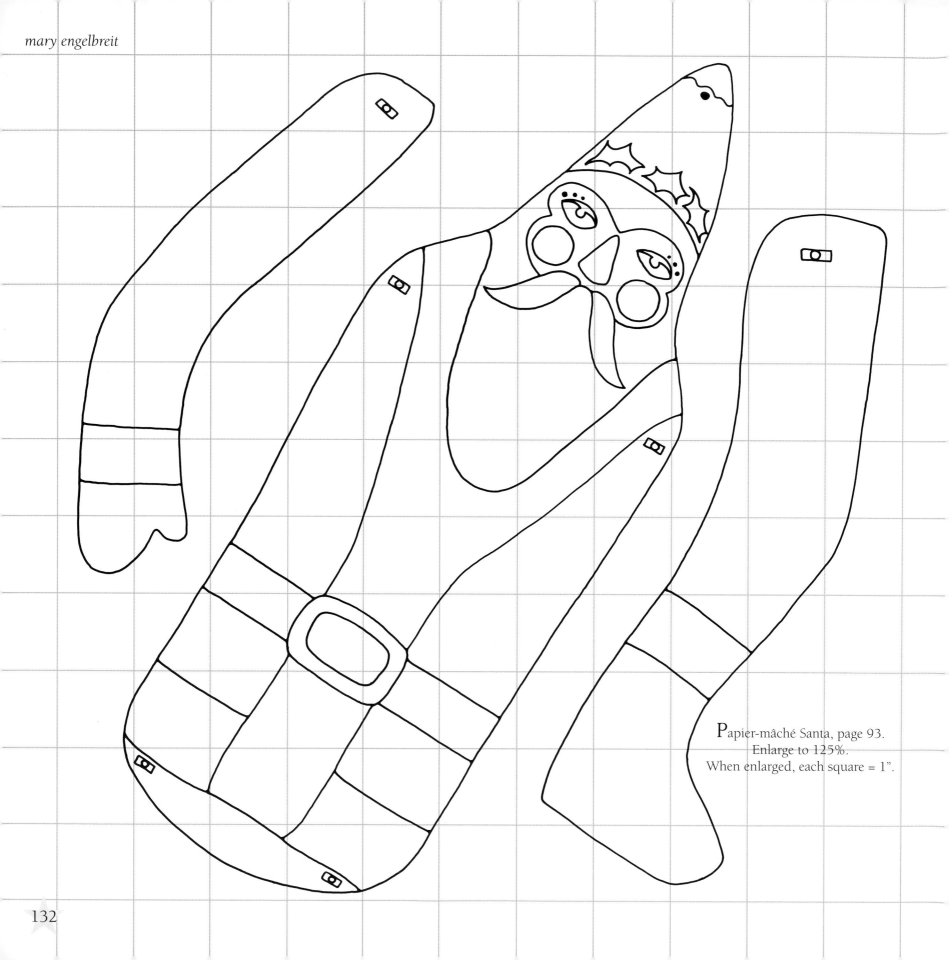

Papier-mâché Santa, page 93.
Enlarge to 125%.
When enlarged, each square = 1".

Credits

Project Designers

Mary Engelbreit
wreath, page 10; decoupaged plate, page 59; painted drinking glass, page 59;
robot tree, page 64; nativity, page 103; table and chairs, page 105;
picture frames, page 112; clock, page 116; gingerbread doll cookies, page 119

Charlotte Lyons
kitchen wreath, page 17; felt stocking, page 33; snowy tree skirt, page 42;
storybook tree skirt, page 47; tabletop tree, page 67; forest angels, page 71;
tie pin, page 82; papiér-mâche Santa, page 93; bean bag Santas, page 101;
reindeer rug, page 101; doll clothes, page 101; puppet theater, page 105;
gingerbread votives, page 106; reindeer brooch, page 108; Christmas album, page 109;
button covers, page 117; child's hat, page 117;
button jacket, page 119; footstool, page 120; appliqúed sweater, page 121;
felt houses, pages 18, 34, 48, 60, 72, 94, 110, 122

Contributing Project Designers

Jeanne Benedict, St. Louis, Missouri
Santas, pages 32, 87

Richard Cottrell, The Antique Garden, St. Louis, Missouri
table decoration, page 55; chair backs, page 58

Teresa Disney/Disney Design, St. Louis, Missouri
tabletop tree, page 65

Veronica Fremont/Fremont Design Studio, Oak Park, Illinois
crystal ornaments, page 115

Kate Gangi/Gangi Design, Oak Park, Illinois
Santas, page 89

Danelle Gardner/The Summer House, St. Louis, Missouri
moss house, page 86

Kathy Gillespie/ Frills, Oak Park, Illinois
stockings, page 30; stars, page 30; tabletop tree, page 30

Maggie Lyons, Oak Park, Illinois
painted box, page 104; village, page 107; sampler, page 116

Mary Morgan, St. Louis, Missouri
tabletop tree, page 66; wreath, page 84

Frank Neal, Michael Mahler/CheapTrx, St. Louis, Missouri
tabletop tree, page 68

Carol Ann Newman, Washington, Missouri
wreath, page 74

Bob Newton/Newton & Kerr Associates, St. Louis, Missouri
tree-topper, page 41; table decoration, page 56

Gary Notwell, Oak Park, Illinois
table decoration, pages 31, 54

Barbara O'Brien/The Silver Garden, St. Louis, Missouri
tabletop tree, page 70

Anne O'Connor/O'Connor Illustration, Oak Park, Illinois
tabletop tree, page 70; black painted shoes, page 108

Darin Sheraka/J. Darin Design, Chesterfield, Missouri
chandelier, pages 55, 115; table decoration pages 55, 77; wreath, page 76

Joseph Slattery, St. Louis, Missouri
door decoration, page 15; tabletop tree, page 69

John Sullivan/Ken Miesner, St. Louis, Missouri
table decoration, page 57

Anna Sunderland, Hutchinson, Kansas
tabletop tree, page 69

Ruth Touhill/Stone Ledge Antiques, Dutzow, Missouri
door decoration, page 14; bear cabin, page 98

Marie Trader, Hinsdale, Illinois
table decoration, page 52

Sonja Willman/The Summer House, St. Louis, Missouri
table decoration, page 50; tabletop tree, page 62

Contributing Interior Designers

Richard Cottrell/The Antique Garden, St. Louis, Missouri
Kathy Curotto/Randolph Mead Antiques, St. Louis, Missouri
Mary Curotto/Randolph Mead Antiques, Kirkwood, Missouri
Sharon Failla/Corner Antiques, St. Louis, Missouri
Kate Gangi/Gangi Design, Oak Park, Illinois
Ken Miesner and John Sullivan/Ken Miesner's, St. Louis, Missouri
Mary Morgan/St. Louis, Missouri
Alice Newquist/Stohl Concepts, St. Louis, Missouri
Bob Newton/Newton & Kerr Associates, St. Louis, Missouri
Gary Notwell, Oak Park, Illinois
Erin Rose Prunty/Roosters, Oak Park, Illinois
Darin Sheraka, Doug Finley/J. Darin Design, Chesterfield, Missouri
Ruth Touhill/Stone Ledge Antiques, Dutzow, Missouri
Marie Trader, Hinsdale, Illinois
Sonja Willman/The Summer House, St. Louis, Missouri

Grateful Appreciation to:

Gail Conklin, Seaside, Florida
Joseph Consolo
Mr. and Mrs. Louis Dennig, St. Louis, Missouri
Mar Gee Farr and Tanner Musso, the Garden Collection, Hinsdale, Illinois;
Father Christmas, page 17
Emmett Johns, St. Louis, Missouri; portraits, page 32
Christopher Radko, New York, New York; tree toppers, page 23
Kay Sorensen, Oak Park, Illinois; nutcrackers, page 16
Ann Swango, St. Louis, Missouri; skinny Santas, page 20
Mary Anne Thomson, St. Louis, Missouri
DuBois and Son Forest Products, Spalding, Michigan
Jean Lowe and Stephanie Raaf/Andrews and McMeel, Kansas City, Missouri
Stephanie Barken and Jackie Landes/The Mary Engelbreit Studios, St. Louis, Missouri

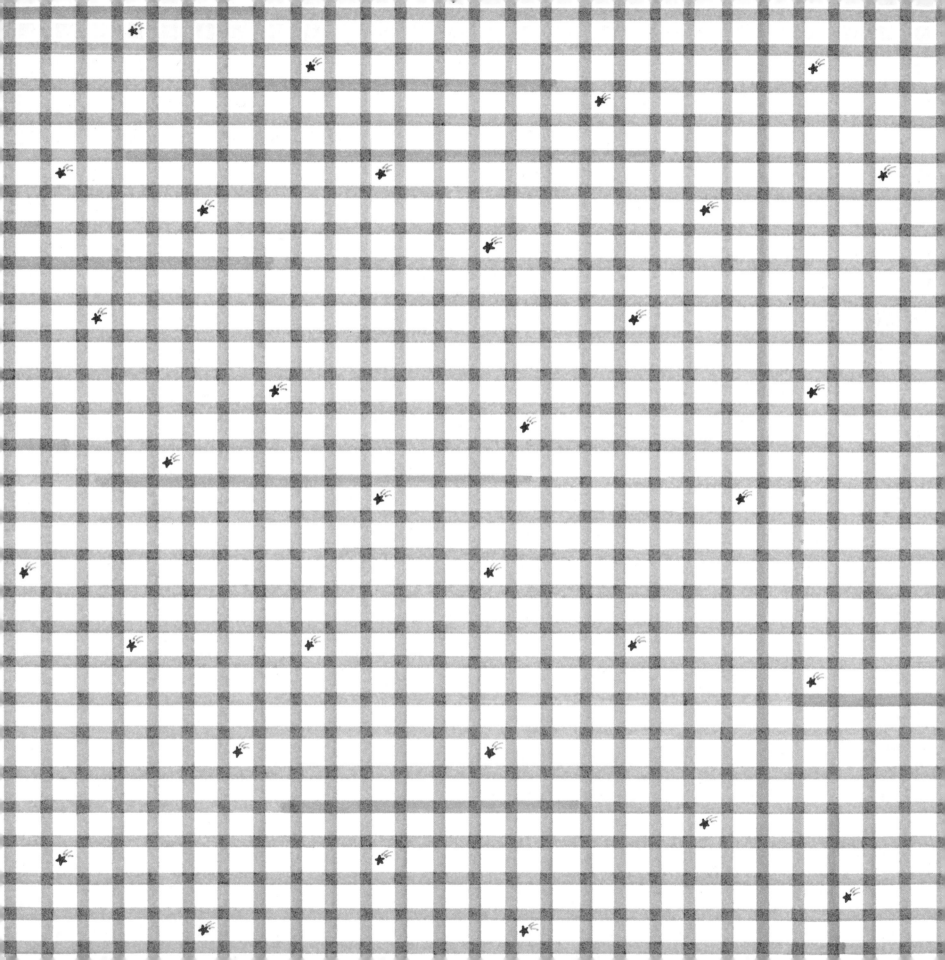